So, How Many of You Are There?

Tales of string quartets and weddings

Alex Averi

Queensland, Australia

Author: Averi, Alex
Title: So, How Many of You Are There?
Edition: First
Publisher: Alexandra K Averi, 2020
ISBN: 9798638500931

Independently published

So, How Many of You Are There?

For Sandra Averi (née Gunn),

who had indomitable enthusiasm

and a song in her heart.

CONTENTS

SO, HOW MANY OF YOU ARE THERE?

Prelude

Each time I arrived early to set up for a quartet gig at a wedding venue, lugging my cello plus my wheeled bag of music folders and music stand, and usually having trekked a considerable distance from the car park, I would find a lone cleaner, waiter, function manager or groundsman wandering about.

"I'm one of the string quartet who are playing today, and I'm wondering where to set up; do you know if some chairs have been set aside for us somewhere, please?"

Their response would inevitably be a mildly disinterested glance, with maybe a raised eyebrow as I staggered under the weight of my oddly shaped pieces of luggage: "So, how many of you are there?" (Variant: "So, how many of youse are there, then?").

I was privileged to play for many weddings in and around the greater Brisbane area during the 1990s and 2000s, when non-church ceremonies underwent a huge increase in popularity. The newly available variety of settings opened up all sorts of possibilities for bridal couples seeking to personalise their special day.

The wedding industry boomed.

Ceremonies were being held at restaurants, gardens, historic houses, wineries, parks, golf clubs and beaches. Civil celebrants were in huge demand, as were limousine companies, caterers, marquee providers, photographers, florists, suppliers of multiple other props and accoutrements—and string quartets.

Those were the pioneering days. The venues and service providers were still in varying stages of gearing themselves up for this new growth industry, and the conditions for the musicians were frequently somewhat rustic.

It had become quite the trendy thing for couples to be serenaded by romantic strings during their ceremony and reception. But many couples had little idea of what a string quartet actually looked and sounded like, and what music choices would work best.

Often, they were blissfully unconcerned about factoring into their planning the chairs and space needed for the musicians, and some means of essential weather protection for our valuable instruments.

We black-clad musicians would turn up, provide the music, then unobtrusively depart—anonymous and unnoticed by many of the guests, apart from a few who might pause in their conversation to offer some laudatory comments on our way out.

This book is the musician's view of the lighter side of weddings, with all the idiosyncrasies, struggles and hilarity involved in creating the Romantic Effect for bridal couples on their special day.

CHAPTER ONE

Processional

Over the years, I have had all sorts of interesting phone conversations with anxious brides who were trying to organise their perfect wedding. They knew it was trendy to have live music from a string quartet, even if they weren't too sure what a string quartet actually comprised. And if any friends or relatives had quartets at THEIR weddings, well, that settled it.

Some were economisers. With a budget of many thousands of dollars already committed for an extravagant reception, limo, catering, photographer, dresses and all the other trimmings, they would then go all out to save fifty or a hundred dollars from the comparatively insignificant fee for the musicians.

"I want a quartet, but with only three of youse," said one bride.

Sometimes a bride would ask me to quote our trio or quartet fees for various lengths of playing time. We'd then discuss repertoire, and she'd decide on her special music for the ceremony. Then, looking for a bargain, she'd say, "So, how much will it be if just one of you plays?"

I'd try to help brides (or sometimes their mothers) with suggestions for musical choices that would lend a suitable air of dignity and timeless style to their day.

People were sometimes a little intimidated by important-sounding names of long-dead composers. But it was amazing how many "classical" favourites they recognised, once they heard how the tunes went.

The suggestion of Vivaldi's *Spring*, for example, would often draw a blank until I sang, "Da dum dum dum da-da-daaa," down the phone.

"Oh yes, I love that song," would come the happy response.

Many young brides, clearly having been raised on a musical diet consisting solely of chart-topping pop-rock songs, struggled when I asked them what special music they would like for their processional, signing the register, and walking out at the end.

Often, they would be glad to just take our advice on pieces that would work well. Sometimes they suggested their latest favourite blockbuster movie hit or pop song.

I'd often try to dissuade them from such songs, because when you substitute just four string instruments for the full arrangement of band or orchestra plus vocals, the songs aren't going to sound exactly the same as the studio-recorded chart-toppers that they are familiar with.

Often a song's main significance is in its lyrics, which aren't heard when the song is played by a quartet. What's left is frequently a very repetitive riff or chord sequence, which doesn't sound too convincing without those all-important song words. And, although a small number of hit songs make it into the ranks of timeless pop-rock classics, many are eminently forgettable. They have their few months of high-volume airplay and then fade into obscurity. They're not the kind of songs that will make lasting memories.

As well as pop songs, we've had other odd processional music requests, including the *Vegemite* song from that all-Australian TV advertisement, *Highway to Hell,* and *My Philandering Days Are Over.*

Many brides opt to walk in to Pachelbel's *Canon*. It's a popular choice, and a safe one, in that it's easy to stop the music at just the right moment.

And yes, that word is "Canon", a musical term describing the way that all three upper string parts play exactly the same melody, two bars apart. Not "Cannon", the spelling that has made its explosively incorrect appearance on many a printed order of service.

Cellists everywhere shudder at the mention of Pachelbel's *Canon,* because the cello part consists of a "ground bass" line that just repeats the same eight-note sequence over and over again, while the upper parts have all the fun.

But it's actually rather useful for the cellist to be able to look around whilst playing this piece for the processional, in order to keep track of the sometimes erratic progress of the flower girls and page boys, bridesmaids and bride, and to anticipate when to stop the music.

The trick is to watch the for the bride's arrival at the front. We then allow a few more seconds for her to move into position beside the groom and exchange a few private pleasantries, before the celebrant begins to speak.

"One more," I whisper, playing my eight-note sequence yet again, as the bride gets close.

"Another one," I murmur, if the celebrant takes extra moments to adjust the position of the bride and groom, utter some quiet reassurances to steady their nerves, or get the bridesmaids lined up at just the right angle.

Or sometimes everybody moves into place with quickfire military precision, and I can see a time-pressed celebrant preparing to speak much sooner than anticipated. A sudden, pronounced *ritardando* (slowing down) from the cello, along with raised eyebrows and an urgent look, serves as the signal that we need to stop.

On their Big Day, the groom and groomsmen arrive early at the venue, looking self-conscious in their hired suits, and alternating between preoccupied silences and bursts of brittle laughter that betray their nerves.

The guests start arriving, and the celebrant does last-minute checks with those participating in the ceremony.

The quartet begins the background music, and an expectant buzz animates the happily-chatting gathering.

The stage is set.

What we musicians most need to know is the precise cue for when the bride and bridesmaids are ready to start walking in. Usually this involves keeping track of the celebrant as that time approaches, while we are playing the background music.

Some celebrants go out to meet the bride, check that she is ready, then walk back in and announce her arrival. Others stay at the front, promising to cue us when the moment arrives.

However, things do not always go exactly as planned.

Sometimes we temporarily lose sight of the celebrant, who is busy chatting with guests. Excited family members rush up to us while we are playing:

"She's here; start the music NOW!" they announce breathlessly.

They have not remembered that after the bridal car has pulled up outside, several long minutes elapse while the photographer organises the "getting out of the car" photos. Then a few hasty checks are made of dresses, veil and bouquets, before the bridal party line up to make their entrance.

Usually the celebrant's cue works perfectly. But occasionally, things go slightly awry if a flower girl or page boy—or the bride—suddenly gets stage fright.

At one garden venue, the processional route involved a long, winding gravel footpath from the car park through a bush canopy, before the first bridesmaid would emerge into view, leading the final walk around the side of a small lake and onto the ceremony lawn.

The celebrant had made the trek out along the path to meet the bridal car. On her return, she cued us to start the processional music. The guests hushed their chatter and waited expectantly, cameras at the ready.

The piece was Vivaldi's *Spring*, which allowed ample time for the bridesmaids and bride to complete their walk.

But by the time we reached the end of the piece, not a soul had appeared on the footpath.

"*Da capo*!" ("Back to the beginning!"), we whispered to each other, slightly alarmed.

The guests were looking puzzled. The groom looked sick with fright.

The celebrant hastily set off back along the path towards the bridal car, managing a surprisingly efficient speed in her high heels and tight skirt.

We were almost at the end of the piece for the second time, and still there was no action on the processional route.

The celebrant reappeared, looking flustered. Signalling for us to stop playing, she faced the assembled guests.

"The bride is almost ready," she announced a little too brightly, wide-eyed and with a fixed smile. She trotted briskly away down the path again.

The guests chattered nervously. The ashen-faced groom stood uncertainly at his post.

We filled in the awkward minutes with background music, uncertain of what dramas were unfolding in the car park.

Eventually the celebrant bustled back into view, pink-faced and puffing from all her exertions. This time, though, her smile was much more spontaneous.

"The bride had an emotional moment as soon as she began walking, and burst into tears," she hissed to us by way of explanation as she made her way to the front.

During our third iteration of *Spring*, the bridesmaids and bride at last made it along the path and successfully into position. Handkerchief in hand, the bride was still sniffling a bit, but she had regained her composure. Both bride and groom brightened up considerably once that processional walk had been accomplished.

Sometimes the processional music requests get a little complicated. A bride may want one piece for the bridesmaids' entry, then a completely different piece for her own entry.

Occasionally we are also asked for a third piece, to underscore the few seconds it takes for the bride's mother to be formally escorted to her seat.

While this sounds wonderful in theory, it can cause some practical difficulties, especially if we are outside on a breezy day, and need to take a few seconds to adjust the clothes pegs that we employ to secure our music.

Discussing the processional pieces with brides by phone before the day, I always remind them: "Wait until you hear the music change before you start walking."

But in the excitement of the moment, few remember.

Summer-sweltering under the meagre shade of an ailing bare-branched jacaranda tree, we were tucked into a corner of the public walkway that adjoined a Brisbane hotel's riverfront lawn.

The wedding guests milled about on the grass as we played. A few passing weekend-afternoon families with bikes and scooters stopped along the walkway to listen in, offering encouraging remarks.

At the appointed time, the celebrant made her way over to the hotel building, from which the bride and bridesmaids would emerge. Our instructions were that the celebrant would return to announce the bride's imminent arrival, and we would begin the processional music.

A few minutes later, we spied the celebrant walking back across the lawn. We stopped the background music and turned our pages to the bridesmaids' entry piece, re-applying our clothes pegs against the page-riffling breeze.

The celebrant reached the front of the red carpet, turned to make her announcement to the guests—and was startled to see the first beaming bridesmaid only metres behind her, marching along at an enthusiastic pace.

"Crumbs, they've already started!" we muttered.

The celebrant shot us a wordless, horror-stricken look. We hastily began playing.

The other two bridesmaids had followed closely and were already making their way along the red carpet.

Just a few short bars of music would play them to the front, then we would turn our pages ready for the bride's entry.

But all the excitement had evidently caused the bride to forget her instructions about waiting for her cue and walking at an elegantly measured pace.

There she was, legging it briskly across the lawn and onto the red carpet, only a few strides behind the last bridesmaid. She clearly wasn't going to wait for the music to change.

There was no chance of playing the third bridesmaid in. We stopped mid-bar and began the bride's piece before she bolted the rest of the way down the red carpet.

It was Pachelbel's *Canon*. The cello starts it off with that well-and-truly memorised eight-note sequence.

We needn't have worried about turning our pages. She had sprinted to the front long before the end of the first eight notes.

The bride's sister was going to sing *Can You Feel the Love Tonight* at the ceremony, I was informed by phone. Would we play for her?

We play melodic rather than chordal instruments. Unlike guitarists, we don't just read chords from a chord chart, moving the *capo* up and down the neck of our instruments to alter the key as needed. We need to source or write a fully notated string arrangement for any pop or rock song, covering as best we can between our four instruments all of the main riffs, rhythmic patterns and melodic lines that are prominently featured.

Therefore, I needed to know in what key the bride's sister wanted to sing it.

I was checking this for a good reason: we have played for many untrained singers at weddings, and it's a dangerous exercise. We usually get no rehearsal with them other than one quick run-through on the day, when many of the guests are already hovering about. And we can't ever assume that they will be comfortable with singing it in the same key as the original.

Often, they get quite flummoxed when they don't hear the string quartet sounding exactly the same as the full set of guitar, bass, drums, keyboard, and lead and backing vocal tracks that they are accustomed to. They are liable to come in at the wrong time or in the wrong key, and it can be difficult to rescue them.

The bride referred my query back to her sister, whose emailed response was: "Ummm, I don't really know what key the song is in, but my guess is C, because that's mainly what key all songs are in."

She thought that maybe if we all arrived early on the day, we could just work out the right key then.

"I've never performed with an actual string band."

I was organising our booking details for the wedding of a mature-aged couple. They were very particular about what style of quartet music they wanted. "It should be all classical," instructed the bride over the phone.

Assuming that she meant "classical" in its general sense of music written anywhere between the 17th century and early 20th century, I agreed that this was perfectly suited to the sound of a string quartet, reassuring her that I had a vast repertoire of beautiful music by many famous composers including Vivaldi, Bach, Handel, Tartini, Haydn, and Mozart.

(Of these, Tartini, Haydn and Mozart are composers specifically from the defined "Classical period" in the late 18th century.)

"Oh, we don't want anything by Mozart. He's far too late," she ordered.

We had our revenge.

After the ceremony, when the happy couple were having a wonderful time circulating amongst their guests, all of them looking elegant and classy against the backdrop of the sun-drenched gardens and sparkling lake, we sneaked in the well-known *Minuet in G* by Beethoven. It segues perfectly into Dennis Wilson's theme tune for the sit-com *Fawlty Towers*.

We've played this a few times at wedding receptions, while the guests are conversing animatedly at their tables. Suddenly, somebody at a random table gets the joke. We hear a burst of laughter, followed by snatches of "He's from Barcelona," and "Don't mention the war."

But this time, nobody noticed.

We were booked to play for a wedding whose bride and groom were both from Italian families. It was in one of Brisbane's large Catholic basilicas, conducted in a bilingual mix of English and Italian.

The bride's mother had perused our long list of examples of suitable string quartet repertoire. She had specifically notified us that Bach's *Jesu, Joy of Man's Desiring* (which has a stately 12/8 triple-time feel) was NOT to be played. She considered that it sounded "too Irish".

Puzzled at first, we realised that if it were to be played much too fast and in a jaunty Celtic style, it might indeed possibly be mistaken for an Irish jig. Perhaps she'd heard some such variant version somewhere. Perhaps Johann Sebastian Bach had a long-lost cousin called Seamus Patrick Bach.

We were also required to accompany two female relatives for a special vocal item: Andrea Bocelli's *Con Te Partirò*. It had clearly been selected because the original lyrics are in Italian. However, I did wonder at the suitability of *Time to Say Goodbye* for a wedding.

The ladies arrived early so that we could rehearse the song with them. It was just as well, for they had a rather elastic notion of bar lines and counting, and they sang the heartfelt lyrics just the way they felt to sing them—which was slightly different each time.

There was no point in trying to correct them. We just had to make it fit.

Rehearsal concluded, the ladies took their allocated seats directly behind the violinists, and the guests began trickling in.

Twenty minutes to go. We began the pre-ceremony background music.

Nobody had yet sighted the priest. We played on and on, and on and on. Still no priest.

Family members were outside making hasty phone calls. It seemed that the priest had got his times mixed up. The bridal cars were circling the block until the priest could be located.

The assembled guests, who had been chattering happily in the pews, were beginning to wriggle uncomfortably, and a general embarrassed silence descended on the congregation.

We kept going with the background music.

As the clock ticked over to half an hour after the time when the ceremony was supposed to start, we were still playing. The priest had not arrived.

Mid-piece, one of the singers leaned forward. Tapping our first violinist on the shoulder, she whispered urgently, in her beautifully rounded Italian accent, "What's your name?"

"Marie."

"Well, play, Marie, play! Papa Luigi isn't here."

On a blisteringly hot, humid, windless summer day in Ipswich, west of Brisbane, we were playing for a wedding in the gardens of a historic house. Seated on the lawn next to a small rotunda, under the limited shade of a tree, we were stifling in our musician "blacks".

Insects buzzed. The sun blazed relentlessly. Elegantly frocked ladies fanned themselves as they balanced carefully on tiptoes to prevent their stiletto heels from digging into the manicured grass. The groom and groomsmen looked as though they were going to pass out in their hired suits.

The bride, with her two bridesmaids, arrived punctually, and the ceremony got under way.

Framed by the rotunda, with the grass and trees in the background, the bridal party looked very photogenic, despite their frequent recourse to pocket tissues for some discreet brow-mopping.

At last, a late-afternoon light breeze began to bring the first hint of welcome relief.

The bridesmaids, in their matching dresses, carefully coiffured hairdos, makeup, and heat-flushed faces, stood demurely in their appointed spots as the celebrant talked on.

During those quiet, most tender moments when the bride and groom were saying their vows to each other, I overheard a muttered conspiratorial exchange between the bridesmaids:

"Can you feel the wind up yer bum yet?"

With a blissful sigh: "Yeah."

SO, HOW MANY OF YOU ARE THERE?

CHAPTER TWO

Romanze

"It will be so romantic," sighed the bride-to-be happily, as she described to me where her wedding ceremony was going to take place: high atop a cliff on the edge of the Redcliffe peninsula, where a great grassy sweep of parkland overlooks Moreton Bay.

I shuddered at my end of the phone.

That dreaded phrase, "It will be so romantic," is frequently uttered by couples who have chosen a boat, riverbank, creek bed, beach, exposed lawn, garden or hilltop for their ceremony.

In Brisbane's subtropical climate, it is a wonderfully romantic notion to be outdoors, with the sun, the view, the clean fresh air, gorgeous gardens, sparkling water, and photo opportunities galore.

However, if there is no shade available, the relentless baking heat of the summer sun can make things very uncomfortable for the formally dressed guests, as well as causing problems for the musicians' instruments.

Moreover, Brisbane gets its share of rainy days, dry, biting winter westerlies, or tropical summer storms that roar in with gales, lightning, and torrential downpours.

My first question to these couples, therefore, is whether they have a "Plan B" for inclement weather.

I'm not only thinking of their guests and their photos. We musicians must protect our valuable instruments, which cannot be exposed to rain or blazing sunshine.

Our music stands, carrying our weighty music folders, act like sails when the wind is strong. We secure the pages of our music with a tried and true, albeit non-high-tech device: clothes pegs. But sometimes the whole music stand gets airborne and topples over. Piling handbags around the bases of our stands helps somewhat, but there's been many a time when I've had to grab onto my music stand with my feet while playing.

This clifftop-loving bride did not have a "Plan B", but she was sure that everything would be fine.

"We've been up there quite a few times, and it has always been beautiful," she assured me.

The day came, and the sun was shining in a clear blue sky. Out on the bay, yachts scudded across the white-flecked water. The view was spectacular. As I parked my car where the road ended, I thought the weather was going to favour us after all.

However, on stepping out of the car, I was greeted by a brisk south-easterly sea-breeze which, on that hilltop high above sea level, could better be described as a howling gale.

We faced a short walk of what felt like several hundred

metres across unmown grass, to the spot where the wedding would be.

Lugging my cello, my trolley of chairs, and the music case, I leaned into the bracing headwind, imagining us in the role of intrepid, jutting-chinned adventurers trekking stoically towards a new frontier.

There was no level ground. We positioned ourselves the best we could on the grassy slope, at alarming angles and with our chairs wobbling precariously on the uneven terrain.

But the wind was our biggest challenge. Every time we put our music folders on our stands, they blew over.

We triangulated the feet of our stands against the trajectory of their fall, and set our bags around their bases. But every now and then, a particularly strong wind gust sent them flying again.

With multiple clothes pegs pinning the folders to our stands and securing the open pages, we next unpacked our instruments.

As we began playing, a fresh challenge presented itself: the wind gusts kept catching our bows and lifting them clean off the strings. Elegant phrasing and beautifully controlled dynamics went out the window as we fought just to hold on to our bows.

Hair whipping across our faces and eyes watering in the wind, we did our best, occasionally lifting our feet indecorously to hold on to our stands as we played.

Turning our pages and re-pegging our folders, we

serenaded bravely away in the most convincingly joyful, nonchalant and romantic manner that we could muster, as the guests' cameras clicked.

During the ceremony, the celebrant's words were carried away on the wind and went completely unheard by many of the guests.

But none of them minded; they watched the bride and groom lovingly speak their vows to each other, they took photos of the romantic bit when the couple exchanged rings and signed the register, they got to cheer and whistle when the bridal couple kissed, and they were all going on to drinks and dinner afterwards.

Packing up afterwards and retreating to the shelter of our cars, we felt windblown, dishevelled and unglamorous.

But the bridal couple and guests had smiled delightedly the whole time. They were clearly satisfied that their ceremony had been wonderfully romantic.

Dusk was falling as we settled into the corner of the verandah that had been assigned to the quartet, to provide background music for the pre-reception drinks.

Over the parklike grounds of the golf course, the westering sunset glow looked magnificent.

As the evening drew in, the venue staff switched on the lights. A few romantically dimmed overhead bulbs gave a candle-like glow to the verandah, and twinkling fairy lights threaded through the surrounding greenery added a magical effect.

Except in our corner, where the light bulbs weren't working.

Nowadays, the music accessories marketplace has responded to musicians' very real need of small, battery-powered gig lights, to carry in our cases and clip onto our music stands in situations of semi-darkness.

But back then, gig lights were not yet readily available. As the darkness gathered around us, we hunched closer and closer into our music stands, peering at the notes. By sticking to repertoire that we all knew extremely well, we managed somehow.

But it got me thinking.

This was one of several venues where we regularly played, that manifested this syndrome. Every time we were there, over a period of several years, the same thing happened.

The lights would be switched on as night fell.

But in the musicians' corner, the same malfunctioning bulb or two, which never got fixed from one gig to the next—or indeed from one year to the next—would leave us in near-darkness, struggling to read our music.

And so I formulated my Law of Illumination: the one light that doesn't work will always be the one directly above the string quartet.

SO, HOW MANY OF YOU ARE THERE?

The prestige Brisbane city hotel had a manicured lawn area adjacent to the riverbank. In its centre was an imposing flagpole, mounted on a small paved area with inset floodlights that illuminated the flag from below at night.

The wedding ceremony was held in the late afternoon on the lawn in front of the flagpole, with the photogenic backdrop of the river and the Kangaroo Point cliffs.

Our quartet was positioned close by on the grass, next to the flagpole. We played for the ceremony, and then were to continue playing for a further hour while the guests enjoyed pre-dinner drinks and canapés on the lawn.

The sun sets very rapidly in sub-tropical Brisbane, and before long the dusk had deepened dramatically. We looked nervously around for the expected outdoor lighting to come on, as tray-laden waiters threaded their way around the groups of guests.

The outdoor lighting turned out to be a few lonely strands of fairy lights in the bushes edging the lawn—plus those in-ground floodlights that were pointed directly up the flagpole into the night sky.

Our noses were almost touching the pages of our music as we struggled to see the notes. We still had a good twenty minutes to go.

There was only one thing for it. We would have to make use of those vertical floodlights.

Moving our chairs so that we were sitting four in a row, directly atop the two side-by-side glass panels through which the floodlights shone, we adjusted our music stands to hold our music almost vertically, catching what we could of that upward beam of light. It helped to some extent, even though the angle was all wrong.

But what it did achieve most effectively was to give each of our faces that spooky look that you can create by holding a torch under your chin.

None of the guests were taking any notice. They stood in the darkness happily munching, sipping and chatting, oblivious of the four black-clad, ghostly spectres bowing our eerily silhouetted instruments, wraithlike within that skyward shaft of light.

Lighting can present unexpected problems indoors, when it is deliberately and abruptly dimmed to a romantic, rather than practical level.

In many an upmarket restaurant or function room, we would serenade happily away with perfect visibility while the guests arrived. During the pre-dinner drinks, they would mingle and chat, and we would play, in bright, cheery lighting.

Then the moment would come for them all to be seated at their tables, ready for dinner to be served.

An unseen staffer would apply a heavy-handed touch to the dimmer control, and suddenly, in mid-piece, our light source would be reduced to a faint glow.

The venue staff were clearly aiming to create the Romantic Effect during dinner—but they didn't have to read the music on the page.

The wedding guests were enjoying the night-time panoramic view of the city lights, as they stood outside in darkness on the hotel's rooftop balcony for their pre-dinner drinks.

The balcony was not equipped with any outdoor lighting, but on one side a generous glow spilled through closed glass doors from the reception room within.

Upon our arrival on the balcony to provide the pre-dinner music, we had gone looking for chairs.

"There are four of us in the quartet," I had explained to a staffer who was reluctant to let us pillage the function room for seating.

Chairs duly sourced, we had set ourselves up just outside those glass sliding doors. That was the only spot where there was any light to read our music. It also provided some shelter from the evening breeze that was funnelling its way energetically between the high-rise buildings.

Everything on the balcony was going just fine. The

wedding guests stood around in small groups, chatting and enjoying the romantic atmosphere. The darkness of the balcony enhanced the festive bustle and lights of the city below.

We played on in our quartet corner.

That is, until ten minutes before the guests were due to move inside for dinner.

Without warning, a staffer inside the reception room pulled heavy drapes across the glass doors.

Plunged abruptly into pitch darkness, we stopped playing. Consternation erupted amongst the guests, who suddenly couldn't see a thing.

At the swish of a curtain, the golden-glowing, convivial evening setting had been transformed into a bleak, windswept, forlorn outpost. On this exposed rooftop of total blackness, the guests felt abandoned and forgotten.

The confused jumble of guests headed *en masse* towards a crack of light that was barely visible at the rear of the balcony. It turned out to be the door into a hallway that led through to the reception room.

We packed up in lonely darkness.

That wedding reception was going to start ten minutes early, whether the wait-staff liked it or not.

Golf clubs are popular wedding venues. They combine the attractive photo backdrop of sweeping greens and open sky, with swanky indoor reception rooms.

One Brisbane golf course with an upmarket function centre sported a wedding lawn perched at the apex of a grassy incline, very close to one of the greens.

Arriving early for a late-afternoon wedding, I found the red carpet and potted plant decorations already in place, and a lone staffer setting out chairs.

I saw chairs for the guests, and chairs for the bridal couple signing the register, but no chairs for the string quartet.

"Do you know where they would like the quartet to sit?" I enquired.

We agreed on the most practical spot, close to where the celebrant would stand for the ceremony.

"May I use some of your chairs for the quartet, please?"

"S'pose so, how many of youse are there?"

As I placed our chairs, and unpacked my stand, music folders, and cello, the celebrant arrived. We stood chatting quietly.

It was a glorious, peaceful late-summer afternoon. Blue sky, hardly any breeze, and the city skyline set in a majestically romantic backdrop to the lawns and trees.

A few golf buggies whizzed around the course below us. The occasional "thwack" of somebody teeing off resounded in the stillness.

Suddenly, a missile slammed into the chair right next to

where I was standing, and cannoned off onto the grass several metres away.

It was a golf ball, which had been hit with considerable force from the green below us, and which was significantly off target.

Shaken, and clutching my cello more closely, I turned in the direction whence the ball had travelled.

Three laughing young blokes on the green below waved a cheerful "Sorry!" as they careened off down the track in their golf buggy.

Just a few minutes later, I would be sitting in that chair with my cello. That golf ball could have seriously injured me, or worse, destroyed my cello.

I spent the entire gig on tenterhooks, nervously hoping that no more erratic golfers were planning to tee off from the green below while we were playing.

That wedding ceremony was going to look magnificently romantic in the photos. But for the musicians, it was downright perilous.

Navigating busy roads to find a venue on a rainy Friday night is never easy. And when the street directions are accompanied by those fateful words, "You can't miss it," I know I'm going to have difficulties.

Our information was that we were playing as a trio for a

couple's anniversary dinner. Initially, a large Gold Coast golf club had been mentioned, and something about two roundabouts that led to parklands behind the club.

The golf club car park was crowded. Cars and pedestrians were coming and going, and the whole place was in full Friday night family action.

The rain poured down. Dazzled by all the oncoming headlights, I squinted nervously through the windscreen as I drove the full length of the car park. I couldn't see anything that resembled the two roundabouts and parklands.

I was very early for the gig. But I was beginning to get that sick feeling in my stomach that happens when I am completely and utterly lost.

Exiting the car park, I drove back out to the main road, and tried the turning on the opposite side. It led to a deserted, dark street alongside a school. Surely this couldn't be the place.

But the street bore the same name as the golf club. And sure enough, there was the first roundabout … and the second roundabout.

The next instruction was to find the parklands 300 metres further on.

There were no streetlights. There was nothing at all, except for a grassy verge running down to one of the Gold Coast's network of canals.

I noticed a couple of car headlights in the vague area described, in a gravelled parking area next to what looked like a wider part of the grass verge. But, peering into the night, I wouldn't exactly have described the area as parklands, and I spotted nothing resembling any kind of function set-up.

Following the headlights, I could see that one of the cars was a stretch limousine. That looked a little more promising.

Then I found my colleagues, who had successfully navigated their way to the same car park.

The rain had stopped. We set off on foot in pitch darkness across the wet grass towards the water, carrying our instruments, chairs, stands and music. Not a soul was about. The lights of a canal estate twinkled romantically across the black depths of the waterway, but on our side the silence enveloped us.

Ahead of us, in solitary splendour next to the water's edge, appeared one of those small backyard marquees that are cheaply available from hardware stores. Within it, a battery work light was rigged up in one corner, illuminating four people who were busily setting up. This was the place, all right.

But, instead of the expected party preparations, we could see only one small card table decked out with a white cloth and formal dinner service, and dining chairs for two.

"Hello, we're the string trio," we announced, putting down our gear in the only corner of the marquee where there was any space.

A young bloke, nattily dressed in suit and tie, greeted us

cheerfully, and then took off at a trot in the direction of the car park. He was travelling home in the stretch limo to collect his lady. It was his family who were setting up his romantic anniversary *dîner à deux*.

As they added their final touches of a bottle of wine, the covered hot dishes, and an esky containing the cold dessert course, we set up our chairs, music stands, gig lights and music.

Then the family members departed, leaving just the three of us seated with our instruments, under the marquee in the middle of nowhere.

"I've left his car keys on the table: can you make sure he doesn't forget them?" instructed his mother as they left.

It was clear that we musicians were expected to double as security guards until the stretch limo returned.

We sat waiting for a good fifteen minutes. Other than the work light and our own gig lights beneath the small canopy of the marquee, the park was silent, lonely and black. A cold evening breeze was picking up. We huddled into our jackets, and affixed clothes pegs to our music stands to hold the pages in place.

We were to play for two hours. It was going to feel like much longer.

"I guess we'll see the headlights when the limo gets back," we speculated, uncertain whether a grand processional entry piece would be the appropriate thing to play when the anniversary couple came strolling all by themselves across the grass.

It was a slightly awkward evening. Each time we finished a piece of music and paused to turn our pages and re-apply our clothes pegs against the breeze, the sudden silence amplified the intimate conversation at the dinner table, to which we were politely trying not to listen.

We played on heroically for the full two hours, never stopping for more than a few seconds at a time. Acutely aware that we couldn't interrupt the stillness with our usual laughs and banter between pieces, we were trying to minimise those uncomfortable silences that might make the couple feel they were being watched and eavesdropped on.

Punctually, they finished their dinner and rose from the table. Remembering to retrieve the car keys that his mother had left for him, our client ushered his lady out of the marquee, and they sauntered away towards the car park.

Having played them out, we packed up in the now-deserted marquee. We were very cold. The night silence reclaimed the parkland.

Hoping that the family members were planning to return in good time to retrieve their marquee, furniture and tableware, we abandoned the dinner setting and set off in the dark to our cars.

We've played for all sorts of crowds, large and small. But this was the only time we've doubled as security guards and serenaded an audience of two.

SO, HOW MANY OF YOU ARE THERE?

CHAPTER THREE

Pastorale

We were to play for a medieval-style wedding, held at an outdoor function venue on a magnificent grassy sward formed by the sweep of a meandering stream.

Arriving early with my cargo of chairs, music, cello and stand, it took a couple of trips to bring all my gear down to the chosen spot for the ceremony—via a steep, slippery bank. The alternative would have been a long walk, following the creek bed around from the other direction. I chose the inelegant scramble down the bank.

The ceremony was to be held under a magnificent shady tree, which was just as well, for the sun was fierce, and stringed instruments cannot be exposed to the hot sun. The only feasible place for the quartet to set up, partly under the tree and thereby gaining some protection from the sun, was in the stony remnants of the small creek, which in flood times, I was told, flowed right through the middle of the grassy area.

When the chairs were out, my music stand was up, and I was doing a preliminary tune-up of the cello, I became aware of little stinging bites around my ankles. The local ant population had discovered me—and worse, they had discovered my cello spike, apparently thinking it formed a very useful highway for ant journeys into the "f-holes" of my cello.

The other musicians arrived just as I was liberally spraying insect repellent not only on myself, but also on whatever parts of my cello I could spray without causing damage. "Don't put your violin cases on the ground here—it's swarming with ants," I warned them—only to discover that my cello case, which I had carefully propped up against the tree trunk, was already rapidly becoming ant-paradise. Cello in one hand and case in the other, I stumbled around on the uneven ground, searching for a spot that was less of an ant thoroughfare.

Eventually we all settled in. The stony creek-bed was none too stable, but we wriggled in our chairs to dig them into position. Amid clouds of insect repellent, we began playing. The sun was worryingly hot, even under the partial shade of the tree, and flies buzzed everywhere.

Only then did we discover the other hazard—the tree canopy was host to a variety of insects, which took to dropping out of it at frequent intervals, to land on our heads, clothes and instruments. While you're playing you can't stop to swipe at them, and close observers would have seen all of us twitching, wriggling, jerking heads, and making abrupt thrusts with elbows as we played—looking decidedly un-serene, un-romantic, and un-glamorous. Flies and mosquitoes love musicians, because they get free rein to park themselves on areas of exposed skin, and do their worst, until the end of the piece of music, when a general relieved swiping, slapping and brushing dislodges them.

The bridal party were happily oblivious, though. Their guests stood, the ladies uncomfortable in elegant footwear on the uneven grass, swatting absentmindedly at flies. Other than being very hot, they were having a great time.

Out came the champagne afterwards, as the official photos got under way, and everybody else's cameras clicked away too. The insects continued to crawl, swarm, and drop relentlessly on the captive musicians.

The effect must have looked romantic indeed—the green riverbank, the string music wafting on the still summer air, the sun, the carpet of rose petals, the medieval attire of the bridal party, and the delighted, dressed-up guests. Only the musicians and the insects knew how it really was.

Trudging along the winding paths in the botanical gardens, I wished I was having a normal kind of afternoon, like all the casually dressed weekend wanderers who, clutching tourist maps and wearing hats, comfortable shoes, T-shirts and jumpers tied around their waists, strolled, pointed, and clicked their cameras.

I was wearing my musician's "blacks". It was humid and the skies were lowering in threat of a summer storm. My shoes felt uncomfortable, and I was hot.

I was also lost. Back in those early years, navigation wasn't easy in the gardens, where all the paths described great circular loops, and the signposting was minimal—so as not to spoil the natural ambience, I thought, in an effort to be charitable.

The thing about weddings in public parks and gardens is that they never have any chairs. You have to bring your own, and in our quartet I was the one who had organised four nice-looking fold-up chairs stacked on a trolley, for use on such occasions. The trouble is, the cellist also has rather a large instrument to deal with, along with music books and stand, and typically the wedding venue is a very long and hilly hike from the car park.

I have often thought that I could rig up all this gear something like a road train. The trolley-load of chairs, my wheeled cello case, and the small wheeled carry case bearing the set of music folders and stand—and of course my can't-be-without handbag, which doubles as my mobile office (must remember to put my phone on silent when I get there), perched precariously on top. I've had dreams of somehow hooking them all up in sequence, with me providing the pulling-power at the front, rear-view mirrors in place, and a sign affixed at the back that says, "LONG LOAD: IF YOU CAN'T SEE MY MIRRORS, I CAN'T SEE YOU".

I had detoured past the information desk to collect a map. Finding it somewhat difficult to follow, I had struggled off on several false leads and doubled back again, road train in tow. As I rounded a corner that seemed suspiciously familiar, I came across three well-dressed people who looked like they pertained to a wedding.

"I don't suppose you are heading for the same wedding as I am?", I greeted them. We compared notes, and they had already done two fruitless circuits of the pathways without stumbling across the footbridge that the map indicated we were looking for. Perhaps we could walk there together?

After an earnest consultation of the map, we decided that the path we were now on seemed like the right one. They were glancing uncertainly at my various odd-shaped cargo items. "Yes, our quartet regularly plays for weddings," I offered conversationally. "Oh—so how many of you are there?" asked the man. I kept my "not-again" grimace firmly on the inside: "We're a string quartet—that's two violins, a viola, and a cello". They looked a bit vague. They'd find out what a quartet was, soon enough.

My arms were beginning to ache seriously. We made two more wrong turns, crossing and re-crossing the creek twice, before we found a lawn next to a rather picturesque little footbridge, which had to be the spot.

A lady was sitting there on the park bench, next to a fold-up table with nothing on it yet, and an ice-filled esky containing refreshments. Yes, this was the place for the wedding. She didn't know where the quartet was meant to set up: "How many of you are there?".

There was no choice anyway, as only one bit of ground, under a tree at one side of the lawn, was relatively flat. That would have to do. Watched by a curious duck which was pecking around the tree, and which seemed to have no fear of humans, I began unpacking the chairs.

The other players arrived together, and on the way they'd joined up with the celebrant. Alarmingly, they seemed to have found a completely different path from the way I'd come.

I began trading stares with several large water dragons around the lawn and near the creek. They were totally unperturbed by the presence of humans in their territory.

As the guests arrived, with much bustling and greeting, we began playing. This is always a good time for us to settle in, and to get the feel of the venue and the gathering. It was also the time when the local population of enormous mosquitoes discovered us, and they sampled our blood enthusiastically as we played. I'm sure they had a touch of dinosaur in their genes somewhere.

Then the duck found my cello spike, digging into the ground. What a wonderful new playground—the cello spike, four music stands, four chairs, and four pairs of human feet, all in a nice little circle to be investigated and pecked. It continued investigating and pecking throughout the entire ceremony, as the occasional water dragon slunk past, heading for the bushes behind us.

The bride arrived, and the ceremony began. Among the invited guests there was to be a priest who would offer a blessing. His cue was announced—and nothing happened. After an anxious pause, a couple of men disappeared back along the paths to see if he was running late or (surely not!) lost. He never did show up. We speculated about how long he might have been wandering around those gardens in ever-widening confused circles, and wondered if he would ever be seen again.

Our instructions for immediately after the ceremony were to play the *Londonderry Air* (the bride was from an Irish family), and then to take a ten-minute break while two belly dancers performed (the groom was of Middle-Eastern origin).

We duly completed the Irish cultural contribution, but then there were urgent gestures and whispers for us to keep playing. Frenzied activity was going on behind the trees, where the belly dancers were supposed to be secretly getting ready for their surprise item. It transpired that they had forgotten to bring the batteries for their CD player, and a mercy dash was under way.

It must have been twenty minutes later that, no batteries having been found, the celebrant came to their rescue, offering the batteries from her small PA unit. At last the belly dancers sashayed forth to take centre-stage. Even their loud music didn't faze our duck, which continued to scratch around at our feet. The water dragons looked on bemusedly from a safe distance away, by the creek.

We never did start playing again. The delays and fill-in playing during the battery crisis had finished our allotted time. We packed up and tried to sneak out quietly, as the affronted duck complained about losing its new playthings, and the audience participation part of the belly dancing was in full, self-conscious swing.

Struggling back to the car with my road-train, which was a little unstable because I had packed the chairs carelessly in my haste, I wondered why we do it. But I knew. These times are priceless and I wouldn't trade them for the world.

SO, HOW MANY OF YOU ARE THERE?

The wallaby eyed me warily as I clattered my way down the walking track to a lookout over a lake—part of the catchment area for Brisbane's Enoggera dam—in a large national park. It was early on a Sunday morning in spring. A slight mist still hung over the water and trees, with the promise of a clear blue day to come. It was perfectly, peacefully still, except for the morning chorus of the many native birds that populate this bushland.

The wallabies here were obviously used to people. The circular walking track, just behind the park headquarters, is accessed through a double gate to protect the wildlife, and it is a popular spot for visitors. Mind you, most visitors don't make their noisy way down the track soon after dawn with a road train of musical equipment in tow.

As I bumped my gear down the first of many steps set into the track, the wallaby sat bolt upright, ears swivelling and nose twitching. This was a different sort of interruption to its morning routine.

I hadn't had many opportunities to get up close and personal with wallabies. Feeling delightfully alone and with no onlookers to think I was being foolish, I stopped and spoke to it. Something in its attentiveness, and its intelligent, brown eyes convinced me that it understood every word I said.

As I chatted happily away to my exquisite, miniature

friend, several more wallabies appeared. They popped up from behind rocks and amongst trees, and watched curiously, heads cocked sideways as they sized up the situation. This was going to be a wonderful morning, I thought as I moved slowly on down the track, trying to minimise the noise of my road train, so as to avoid startling these delicate little animals.

As usual, I had arrived very early. I am always concerned about delays on the roads or difficulties in finding venues, so I regularly allow myself much more time than I need. On this day, I had a glorious twenty minutes to myself. The wallabies silently observed me from close by, the birds squawked and trilled all around, and the lake, overhung with bush, was darkly mirror-still. These magical, thoughtful, times are few, and I treasure them.

A staff member from the park headquarters came down the path, to check who was there and if everything was all right. After a lengthy discussion about which way the bride was going to walk in and where the guests would stand, I was asked to relocate our chairs.

Some tactful negotiating was called for, as the spot where they wanted the quartet to sit was an impossibly tiny area into which we could not fit. The staffer struggled to understand why we couldn't play our instruments sitting all squashed together in a row. "Well, how many of you are there?".

My colleagues arrived. The wallabies kept a safe distance, but they were watching every move. By now the magical morning mist was dissipating, and a bright sun made the water and the dew sparkle.

The celebrant arrived, the guests assembled, there was loud chatter, some of the guests and wedding party lit cigarettes, and the wallabies hastily retreated to the safety of the bush.

The wedding guests were having a great time, but they didn't seem to have any awareness of our background music or the tranquil setting. I felt somehow guilty at being a part of the noise and uncaring-ness that was violating the natural wonder of this place.

This ceremony felt short and perfunctory, and without the meaningfulness that is so much a part of the fabric of many other weddings that we play for. The stillness and the mystery of the early morning were well and truly banished.

But my day couldn't be spoiled. I had experienced a special, solitary time, in the dawn silence of the bush. And I had made friends with some wallabies.

From Brisbane's Mount Cotton, you can see right out across Moreton Bay, as far as Stradbroke Island. Our quartet regularly played for weddings in the magnificent gardens that occupied a commanding position high on the hillside, but on this occasion the bridal couple had chosen the summit of the hill for their ceremony. Everyone was to gather at the gardens, from where two buses would drive us all to the top of the hill.

The guests chattered in small, uneasy groups. Amid nervous jokes, we waited with them for our transport for the big climb to the summit.

Two twenty-seater buses eventually pulled up, and we all piled on. I clung desperately to my cello case, as the asphalt road quickly became a dirt track, and our bus negotiated a series of impossibly tight zig-zag corners.

All my fond thoughts of a jolly funsters' singalong with the partying guests quickly evaporated as, engine roaring, the bus tackled near-vertical gradients that I thought we'd never survive. The sheer slope of the hill dropped away below us, seemingly only inches from the wheels. We sat, white-faced and tight-lipped, barely managing to breathe. Gears grinding, the bus inched upwards ever more slowly, until I feared we would begin rolling backwards, only to tumble off the edge and forever downwards, through the suddenly menacing bush on the slopes below.

After a five-minute ride that lasted for several hours, the slope abruptly levelled out, and we were there. With all the heroic, chin-jutting bravery of an epic band of survivors, we alighted from the buses. Noisy chatter broke out, there was relieved laughter, and we all busily set about catching up with our lifetime friends of just a few minutes.

It was a short walk over steep, rough ground up to the hilltop, where there was just an uneven, grassy slope, ringed with bush. But it was worth it. The view, spectacular from the gardens below us, was awe-inspiring from the summit.

It is a very unusual sensation, playing on steeply sloping terrain. Marie—the first violinist—and I were both sitting sideways on the slope. Andrea and Joan—the second violin and viola players—were facing downhill, bracing themselves with their feet as they perched at an extraordinary angle on the edges of their chairs.

Sitting sideways presented a completely new challenge for our bodies' circulatory systems. After only ten minutes my downhill leg was completely numb, and the pins-and-needles in my downhill foot rendered it completely useless in its bracing-and-propping-up function. My spine twisted unnaturally, as my middle ear instructed it to find the perpendicular. The plastic chairs felt about as comfortable as slabs of concrete. The sight of me standing up and shaking out my numb leg every few minutes between pieces must have looked a trifle unusual, but it helped.

Marie gave up first, and moved her chair around, into the marginally preferable downhill-ski-run position. Then I also rotated my seating angle a few degrees, although this sitting-in-a-row mode made it a little difficult to watch and hear each other while we played. Our heavy music folders wobbled precariously on the unstable music stands.

Mercifully, the bride arrived punctually from her car ride up the hill, and the ceremony was a brief one. We played for another quarter of an hour or so while the guests enjoyed a celebratory champagne. Then it was a hasty pack-up for the trip back down in the buses.

The downhill trip was less frightening, because now we knew what to expect. It is an extraordinary experience, though, to sit at the front of a bus that is picking its way down a slope so steep that through the windscreen you see only the bush dropping away vertically, terrifyingly, into the depths below.

It was with great relief that everybody moved into the marquee in the gardens below, to begin the wedding reception. Musicians and guests at a wedding don't normally expect a fun-park thrill ride to be part of the package. But it was worth it, for the awesome sensation of being isolated on the roof of the world, with a million-dollar view as a backdrop for the ceremony. And it certainly broke the ice among the guests.

After a rainy morning, the ground was puddled and soggy. The afternoon sun had made a gallant appearance, but menacing storm clouds were massing to the west. We hoped those clouds would stay away until the outdoor ceremony was completed.

Andrea, one of our violinists, was in my car for the long drive to a winery venue on the north-western outskirts of Brisbane. We'd played there before and were already familiar with its obscure driveway entrance.

But arriving rather early, we hadn't previously encountered the closed farm gate that now barred our way.

Andrea, in a display of practical farming savvy, offered to hop out and open the gate. The only problem was that the ground was muddy and Andrea, who has impeccable taste in shoes, was wearing delicate high heels topped with black mesh and diamantés.

She managed, with mincing tiptoe steps and much

giggling, to traverse the dirt track with the unhooked gate, and then to re-fasten the gate behind the car after I drove through. She picked her way back along the track to the car, and anxiously checked her shoes. Having survived the mud remarkably well, they still looked glamorous.

The risk of ruin to Andrea's shoes turned out to be a portent of things to come.

The outdoor ceremony passed uneventfully, graced by the sun throughout. In fact, it was beautifully photogenic. The gardens sparkled, their sprinkling of leftover morning's raindrops reflecting the light in nature's own version of diamantés.

The colours of the sweeping, pastured valley below us with its backdrop of distant hills looked more intensely green against the looming, stormy, green-gray horizon.

The air was forebodingly still as the late-afternoon humidity gathered.

Relieved that everything had gone smoothly thus far, we relocated to the indoor dining area after the ceremony. The guests piled in, and a noisy, happy reception got under way as the evening drew in.

Playing away in our dimly lit corner, we began to be aware of intermittent flashes of incandescent white light. Only a few short seconds later came the rumbles, then loud cracks of thunder.

Those storm clouds had been steadily moving in and were now right overhead. Out of the stillness, a vicious wind kicked up. The near-cyclonic gusts lashed at the canvas awnings along the outside face of the building, driving the pelting rain horizontally through the gaps it found between the folding glass doors below.

Murmurs of initial alarm interrupted the festivities. The guests seated along the exposed side of the room were getting wet. Staff hurried to move their tables closer into the room.

We played on, protected under a solid part of the roof. The storm's roar was deafening.

The party erupted back into full swing. Nobody was going to be deterred by a mere summer storm.

After the first hour of the reception, we were due to finish playing. As we packed up, we could hear the rain driving down relentlessly outside.

We opened the exit door to make a dash for it to the car park.

We were greeted with a river of ankle-deep, fast-flowing water blocking the full length of the pathway.

"My shoes!" wailed Andrea.

Retreating back inside, we figured there was only one thing to do. Shoes off and trouser legs rolled up, we intrepid musicians, laden with our instruments and bags and clutching our shoes, sallied bravely forth in bare feet to wade unceremoniously through the flooded darkness.

Andrea's exquisite mesh-and-diamanté shoes had survived the mud at the farm gate. But they would have been no match for that storm.

It was one of those glorious winter days that Brisbane does so brilliantly. The sky was a clear, cloudless blue, and the sun was warming things up nicely after a chilly night. The wind had just enough of a biting edge to remind you that it was indeed winter.

My mother was at that time our quartet's first violinist. She and I had set off in my car for a marathon day of two three-hour wedding gigs. The first was outside Maleny, in the Sunshine Coast hinterland, and the second was in the Brisbane city centre. We had only an hour between weddings, and it would take us most of that time to drive from one to the other. But Mum was in the middle of six rugged months of chemotherapy treatment, and I worried that the day would be too exhausting for her.

Armed with a thermos of coffee and some muffins, we took our time to navigate the breathtaking drive through the Glasshouse Mountains to Maleny. We found the function venue easily, on a hilltop with a spectacular view over the range, and then sat in the car for an energy-gathering coffee break. I treasured these rare times of laughter and talk, alone with Mum. By then we both knew, although it was unspoken, that she only had months to live.

When the other players arrived, we all walked in together. But we discovered that the function room we had seen from the roadside main entrance was not where this wedding was to be held. A staff member led us on a trek down some stairs, through a hallway, down some more stairs, along a path, and then to a steep descent on irregularly spaced narrow steps, down what felt to us like a sheer cliff face.

We were all carrying instruments, stands and music bags, and I worried about Mum's limited energy reserves being too depleted by the time we got there. But her inherited Highland stubbornness was asserting itself. She laughed and joked, and she was going to make the most of this adventure.

Finally, we reached a large timber deck, built around two sides of a reception room that clung precariously to the hillside. The ceremony was to be held in a gazebo perched next to it on a tiny piece of level ground.

We set up as instructed, on the side of the deck facing the gazebo. The mountain wind was gusting coldly, and we were on the side away from the sun.

On went our jackets, and out came the clothes pegs (low-tech but effective) that we use to secure our music. The whistling wind cut right through us, and we felt our hands and feet going numb. Our eyes were watering, our hairstyles were in disarray, and we shivered miserably. Around the corner, sheltered from the wind and in full sunshine, the guests gathered, enjoying pre-ceremony drinks.

We knew we couldn't keep this up for the full three hours. "Would you mind if we moved around the corner out of the wind?" we asked through chattering teeth. "Not until after the ceremony," answered the function manager. She laughed chirpily. "Yes, we know this is a bit of a wind funnel, but you're out of the way here."

"A bit of a wind funnel" was putting it mildly. Our next, unanimous repertoire choice was Vivaldi's *Winter*.

Somehow we got through the ceremony part, and then played for another half an hour or so before the function manager decided that we would no longer be in the way if we moved around the corner.

Thankfully, and somewhat dishevelled, we resumed playing in our new location, and immediately felt better. The view was stunning, and as we thawed out under the benevolent sunshine, things were definitely looking up.

Mum was tiring, but she was determined not to give in. However, the biggest challenge was yet to come. After we finished our three hours of playing and packed up, we faced the daunting climb back up that mountainside with our gear.

Mum made it to the top unaided, still tapping into that life-zest she had, to find the fullest enjoyment in every experience.

We sat in the warmth of the car, fortifying ourselves with coffee from the thermos, combing our hair back into some semblance of respectability, and giggling at being nearly blown off a hillside while trying to look elegant, effortless and insouciant.

That's what I remember most clearly about that day. Even though I was worried about Mum, and we froze in the wind, and we had such a difficult hike down the hillside and back, it was a rich, shared time that was full of laughter.

The warm sunshine in that blue forever-sky made it seem like the whole world sparkled; the view from the mountain range made us feel a tiny part of the grand scheme of things; and everything was going to be all right.

SO, HOW MANY OF YOU ARE THERE?

CHAPTER FOUR

Barcarolle

"We're getting married on the beach", said the bride over the phone.

"You mean, on the actual sand part of the beach?" I asked, heart sinking. Sand, sun, wind and waves at close range aren't a great combination for players of string instruments.

"Yes, it will be so romantic," she enthused. The chosen spot was a narrow strip of sandy beach, where the Gold Coast's narrow Spit faces back towards the mainland across the calm Broadwater.

I enquired whether she had a "Plan B" in case it rained.

She did not, but she was sure that everything would be fine.

"After all, it's summer," she explained. There were some low trees behind the beach that people could stand under, or guests could park close by and go to their cars for shelter if need be.

"That won't help the musicians if there's a storm," I thought, knowing too well the ferocity of subtropical summer storms in South East Queensland. I decided to arrive extremely early on the day in order to grab a prime parking spot, for a rapid exodus with our instruments at the first sign of rain.

The day came, and my fears proved well-founded.

It was a humid late afternoon. Ominous dark grey clouds, with the tinge of green that presages a severe tropical thunderstorm, were gathering over the hinterland to the west.

I parked my car, unloaded my gear, and threaded my way through the thin strip of scrubby bush to the appointed spot on the beach. A lone family member, who had been entrusted with the setting-up duties, was already on site with a small card table, plastic chairs for the bridal couple and quartet, and a couple of large eskies containing the post-ceremony libations.

The only other occupant of that part of the narrow beach was a topless sunbather. She clearly wasn't part of the wedding, and I guessed she would soon move on when her solitary spot was invaded by a troupe of much more substantially clad wedding guests.

The sand was spongy and soft under my feet. As the cellist, I found this particularly concerning. I was not keen for my cello spike to bore its way deep into the sandy depths.

I asked the family member if he had a tarpaulin or groundsheet to put down underneath our chairs, to prevent them from sinking into the sand. I had previously mentioned this on the phone to the bride, and she had assured me that it would be taken care of.

"Yes, we've thought of that," he replied brightly.

He produced two small, flimsy cotton tablecloths: one for the quartet, and the other for the bridal couple's chairs and table for signing the register.

Unfolding the tablecloths with a flourish, he placed ours on the designated spot. As the wind caught it, the thin cloth immediately flipped up and threatened to escape along the beach.

We secured it by placing the four quartet chairs at each corner. I unfolded my music stand and pushed it down into the uneven cotton-lined sand.

The black-green cloud mass over the hills loomed a little closer. I didn't have a good feeling about this gig.

My colleagues arrived, and we did the best we could to set up on our tiny square of cotton cloth. Mercifully, a pre-storm cloudy haze had begun to block the sun's rays somewhat.

The wind was picking up. With multiple clothes pegs pinning our music folders in place, we began playing as the first of the guests appeared out of the tree line to gather on the sand.

They did their best to decently avert their eyes from the topless sunbather, who hadn't moved. She appeared to be oblivious of the activity going on around her.

The celebrant arrived. She eyed the approaching storm clouds dubiously.

"I'll speak very quickly," she said. "Hopefully we can get them married before the storm hits."

As we awaited the bride's arrival, lightning flashes flickered within the cloud mass, and thunder rumbled steadily. Handel's *Fireworks Music* seemed to suit the mood.

At last, the topless sunbather got the hint and left the beach.

Then it was time for a few brief measures of Pachelbel's *Canon*, just enough for the bridesmaid and bride to traverse the narrow strip of sand.

The lightning show was looking increasingly spectacular and getting alarmingly close. The thunder became insistent and angry. The celebrant, true to her promise, conducted the ceremony at her fastest-ever rate of words per minute.

The couple said their vows, exchanged their rings, and were declared husband and wife. We played their chosen music as they signed the register.

The first few specks of rain fell. We knew we had to pack up our instruments.

But it was the wind that decided things. As we debated whether we could wait long enough to play a few bars of the final processional piece, the wind swirled violently in ahead of the storm. It blew our stands over, almost snatched away the wedding certificate, and whipped up the edges of our tablecloth.

The specks of rain began to intensify into heavier drops.

The guests fled to the cover of the trees, followed at speed by the bride and groom. Snatching up her bag and paperwork, the celebrant brought up the rear.

There would be no processional. We packed up our instruments in record time, grabbed our music stands and folders, and raced to our cars, reaching their sanctuary just as torrential rain began to drench the beach.

Struggling along the riverside path at Newstead with my trolley of chairs, bag with music books and stand, and cello in tow, I could see why the small white rotunda ahead of me was a photogenic choice for a wedding ceremony. It was picturesquely situated over the water, right on a bend in the Brisbane river. It faced inwards to a manicured lawn on its landward side, and behind that was the historic Newstead House and gardens.

The sun was bright, and the autumn sky was clear blue with the merest scattering of powder-puff clouds.

I staggered up the final steep climb to the lawn area, arms weary from having carried my heavy load a considerable way from where I had parked my car.

Inside the rotunda, a small card table and two chairs were already in position for the signing of the register. Funnelling through this exposed spot, the river breeze whistled with gale-force intensity.

Backing my cello case carefully up against a side-post lest it blow over, I went through the usual routine of setting up our chairs, my music stand, and the music folders.

The celebrant arrived. We had to shout our greetings to each other as the wind carried our words away.

The celebrant unfurled a crisp white cloth for the card table, but a gust grabbed it, pulling it skywards. Clutching her end as she wrestled for control, she wondered aloud if the unadorned card table might have to suffice this time.

My colleagues arrived and joined in the set-up. The pages of our music folders flapped wildly on our stands, around the bases of which we had piled our bags as ballast.

We began the background music, wrangling multiple clothes pegs, blinking our windblown hair out of our eyes, and fighting to keep our bows on the strings.

The guests gathering on the lawn in front of the pergola looked glamorous and festive. Standing there, they were in a sheltered spot, untroubled by the savage wind.

At the time when the ceremony was due to commence, we watched the celebrant make her way out through the gardens to the car park from where the bride would arrive.

She was gone for quite some time. We played on.

And on.

The celebrant returned, a determined smile on her lips and a flinty glare in her eyes. Clearly making a heroic attempt at reining in considerable frustration, she lined up the increasingly shaky-looking groom and groomsmen in their appointed spots.

At last, the bride was ready to make her appearance. We began the processional.

The bridesmaids made their controlled way along the red carpet and into the rotunda. Nobody else appeared.

We reached the end of the piece and went back to the beginning, sensing that further dramas must be unfolding in the car park.

After what seemed like many more long minutes, the bride appeared, one elbow securely anchored in her father's grasp. She held her bouquet in one hand and clutched a champagne flute in the other, waving it in a celebratory way towards the guests as she passed by them.

She was flushed and swaying slightly in the warm sunshine.

"Looks like she's eaten nothing all day," we speculated.

The celebrant spoke efficiently and gunfire-rapidly.

The bride giggled her way through the vows, then plonked herself down with obvious relief for the few minutes it took to sign the register.

Glad that she'd at least made it through the ceremony, we played the "walking out" music.

We then faced a rapid pack-up. The couple had also engaged us to board a paddle steamer with the guests, to play background music for the first hour of their river cruise reception. After playing for the afternoon tea, we were to be dropped off back at the pontoon, before they continued their cruise with the dinner and speeches.

We had less than ten minutes while they took group photos, to move with our instruments and gear over to the pontoon near to the rotunda, ready to board first so that we could set up and serenade the guests as they came up the gangway.

Within those few minutes, I also faced a hasty dash back along the riverside path to my car, to drop off my trolley of chairs.

Leaving my cello and bags with the others, I set off at a trot. Half running, half walking back, I could see the paddle steamer in position at the pontoon. Two of my colleagues were boarding, and one waited with my gear.

I ran faster. I would like to say that I sprinted with athletic grace, but that would be a grossly untrue exaggeration for this most unsporting cellist.

Puffing and flustered from the exertion, I made it on board with only a minute or two to spare before the guests began filing aboard.

The paddle steamers that ply the Brisbane river are elegant, gracious reminders of a bygone era. Sitting in the spacious, wood-panelled interior, next to its wide-open doors to the deck, views and breezes, we settled happily into our serenading role.

Some guests sat at tables and talked, others wandered around the upper and lower decks. The water sparkled under the sunny sky. The wide, stable boat carved its majestic way smoothly through the water.

Except for each time it passed another boat on this very busy waterway. Then the long wake would cause the distinctive sideways rolling that startles landlubbers until they begin to gain their sea legs.

For us musicians, this was a new experience. Feet planted firmly, we rode the swaying deck as we played, with only the occasional rescuing grab at our music stands.

We felt some affinity with Handel's 18th century orchestral musicians, who famously piled aboard barges to serenade King George I and his royal party for hours on end with repeated renditions of the *Water Music* suite, during their picnic cruise up and down the Thames.

Such was the way of things before the invention of recording and ghetto-blasters. There really is something fresh, immediate and visceral about live music, especially aboard a riverboat.

Not long afterwards, we found ourselves back on the Brisbane River, this time chugging aboard an ex-ferry boat. Some of these historic, quaint little tub-shaped craft still ply the river as ferries. Others have been converted for private use.

We had boarded one such boat from a public pontoon, along with the celebrant and an excited crowd of wedding guests.

Finding our four assigned chairs on the small, low stern deck next to the gangway, we unpacked our instruments and stands. Squeezing into our places, we began playing while guests continued to push past us as they came aboard.

Cruise staff greeted the guests with alcoholic refreshments, as they found their vantage points along the front and top decks. The ceremony was to be conducted aboard the boat as it cruised the river.

Moored at the pontoon until the bridal couple arrived, the boat's engine idled. Amidst the thrum of the motor and the choking diesel fumes, the guests helped themselves liberally to drinks as they awaited the bride and groom.

We played and played.

The guests were having a marvellous time. Their voices increased in volume and hilarity proportionately to the amount of time spent aboard the boat and the number of drinks consumed.

Eventually the bridal couple appeared on the pathway from the riverfront parkland. We hastily turned our pages to play their entry music, drowned out by the enthusiastic applause and raucous cheers of the guests.

At last they were safely aboard. The crew cast off, and the boat was under way.

The ceremony began, with the celebrant bracing herself halfway up the gangway between decks, the couple standing near us on the lower deck, and the by now only half-concentrating guests filling up all the vantage points.

A mighty cheer signalled the couple's official launch into married status, and then the celebrations kicked into high gear.

It was only as the boat reached its full speed in the river channel that we appreciated just how low the stern sat in the water, and just how close to the waterline our seats were. Keeping a watchful eye on the small puddles that were forming near our feet in the open corners and gang-plank railings where the water splashed in, we really were getting up close and personal with the river.

The boat cruised a long way up-river before making the turn for the cruise back towards the pontoon. Seeing Brisbane from the "brown snake", as its river is affectionately known, offers a whole new perspective of the city.

Our view from the open back of the boat was splendid. So splendid, in fact, that occasionally one of us would miss the odd repeat in the music as we stole preoccupied glances at the unfolding panorama along the riverbanks.

Despite the rolling of the boat and the perilously close splashes of water, we counted ourselves lucky. We were only there as the hired musicians, but our bonus was a free river cruise while we played.

Several of Brisbane's riverside restaurants and cafes make the most of their outdoor lawn areas to host weddings and functions.

The splendid photo opportunities of the river backdrop are somewhat compromised by the foot traffic on the adjoining public walkways that line the riverbank. Weddings attract an enthusiastic, curious crowd of extra spectators amongst the passing parade of lycra-clad joggers, young couples with strollers, weekend fitness enthusiasts in sports shoes and daypacks, and families on scooters and bikes.

One such venue was flanked on its landward side by the restaurant's carpark, screened only by a thin hedge.

The afternoon was summery and spectacular, and the restaurant staff were at capacity, serving a brisk indoor trade as well as the large crowd of wedding guests on the outside lawn.

Arriving early, we had set ourselves up in our usual spot, tucked snugly in between the wedding marquee and the narrow strip of garden in front of the hedge.

The formally dressed guests filled the rows of outdoor chairs and stood around the sides and back of the lawn, sporting sunglasses and fanning themselves in the heat. Flies buzzed. Harried function staff bustled to and fro.

The public walkways were crowded. Dawdling onlookers watched and pointed as the bride entered.

The celebrant's PA-boosted voice had to compete with the high-revving comings and goings of several cars on the other side of the hedge.

"... I am duly authorised to solemnise this marriage," intoned the celebrant to the hushed guests.

"Eh?" yelled someone in the carpark as car doors slammed.

An indistinguishable reply came from a different direction behind the hedge.

"If anybody has any objection to this marriage, now is the time to say so," came the official words from the celebrant.

"Yeah, OK ... Nah," was heard from the car park.

The dry, summer-scorched grass crunched under our feet as we made our way across Captain Burke Park, on the Brisbane riverfront underneath the Story Bridge.

The ceremony was to be on the lawn area next to a pontoon, where a river cruise boat was already moored in readiness for the wedding party and guests to embark for their reception afterwards.

The staff from the cruise boat company bustled about on the grass, setting out white chairs, potted plant decorations, a couple of tables with white cloths, and a red carpet to roll out for the landlubber ceremony part of the function.

There was only scant shade from a few straggly trees, but we found a spot that offered at least some protection for our instruments. Could the quartet please use some of their chairs?

"Yes, zat will be fine," said César, one of the cruise boat staff, in a thick South American accent. "How many of you are zere?"

A pleasant breeze coming off the river helped to offset the baking heat of the sun. But it didn't quite manage to dispel the pungent odour from several overfull rubbish bins situated near the public barbecue areas nearby.

The guests began to arrive, and we serenaded away with

the background music. The riverfront setting, with its view of the city directly across the river, looked very festive.

Except for those smelly bins, and the blowflies that buzzed around them in a most unromantic way.

But these function staff were prepared for all contingencies.

César, who by now was looking dapper in his smart uniform shirt over black trousers, nipped inconspicuously around the bins, wielding a spray can of deodoriser.

Having done a preliminary lap with his spray can, he then returned with several pale pink bedsheets, which he proceeded to drape over each bin as camouflage.

Although these lumpy, monolithic pink structures looked somewhat incongruous against the natural setting of the park, I had to admit that, viewed in context with the red carpet, white chairs and potted plants, they were a better sight than the overflowing rubbish bins.

During the ceremony, César made a few more discreet rounds with his deodoriser spray whenever the unpleasant smell threatened to again break forth from beneath its pink coverings.

Everyone worked well together to make it a special occasion for the bridal couple: the cruise boat crew with their outdoor furniture and decorations, the celebrant, and our quartet.

But César, with his pink sheets and deodoriser, provided perhaps the most valuable but least applauded service on the day.

SO, HOW MANY OF YOU ARE THERE?

I had arrived early for a wedding ceremony in the gardens of a restaurant at bayside Cleveland. The beautifully tended lawn, fringed by trees and shrubs, gave way to a low line of mangroves along the waterfront.

A stiff sea breeze howled in from the bay. We were to play on a small brick-paved area at the side of the garden, just next to the spot where the bride would begin her walk down the red carpet that the staff rolled out for these occasions.

Nobody was around. There were four chairs set around a small round outdoor table: of that small, rounded, white-painted wrought-iron variety that grace many a private back yard.

I moved the table out of the way, positioned the four white chairs for the quartet, then set about putting up my music stand and organising the music folders.

The winter wind was merciless. Leaves were swirling, clouds were lowering, and we were bereft of any weather protection. I knew it would be one of those ordeals where our handbags would have to double as sandbags around the bases of our music stands.

Crouching down low over one of the white chairs, I drew my black coat closely around me as the wind whistled. Clad in my musician "blacks", I was also wearing black fingerless gloves to keep my hands warm. Hunched tightly over the music folders on the chair, I was trying to prevent the pages from blowing away as I worked through them, bookmarking the day's music selections.

Glancing up, I saw the restaurant's function manager heading directly towards me as she struggled along with the large roll of red carpet.

As she drew closer, I called out a friendly "Hello."

She froze. Eyes popping, her head whipped around and back again, in a double-take that resembled a Disney cartoon.

She dropped her roll of carpet with an involuntary "Oh!", clutching theatrically at her heart.

"Sorry, I thought you'd seen me—I didn't mean to startle you," I apologised, from my huddled position over the white chair.

She mopped her brow with relief as her breathing gradually returned to normal.

"I thought you were a bloody magpie!"

CHAPTER FIVE

Kinderscenen

Small children ramp up the cuteness factor in a bridal procession, leading the way with their baskets of rose petals to scatter along the red carpet.

However, their participation frequently results in unpredictable and erratic progress down the aisle.

Beginning the entry music in many a ceremony, we would look across and spot a tiny flower girl, flushed with excitement and feeling like a princess in her special tulle dress, headband, white frilly socks and sparkly shoes. Or a pint-sized page boy in his miniature version of an adult black suit, tie and polished shoes to match the groom's and best man's, his hair carefully combed and gelled.

Or maybe a little costumed character: at one wedding on an acreage property, the pageboy was a solemnly earnest miniature cowboy, complete with lasso and sheriff badge.

From the children's point of view, this day was looking promising. So far, it was shaping up to be all about them.

Sneaking glances at their progress down the red carpet, we knew to expect anything, and to be prepared for the processional music to take a bit longer than usual.

Some infants would be overcome by sudden shyness as soon as they realised everybody was looking at them, standing riveted to the ground at their starting point. Some of them would burst into tears from sheer terror at the prospect of their solo walk through that impossibly long gauntlet, lined on both sides with a host of unknown faces and pointing cameras.

An embarrassed mother or bridesmaid would try to cajole them into walking. Sometimes an extra adult had to unofficially join the procession, carrying the whimpering little page boy or princess down the aisle.

Other children would set off confidently enough, as they had practised. But halfway down the aisle, they would spot a favourite aunty, uncle or cousin, and make an unscheduled detour to receive admiration and be photographed.

Then there were those fearless youngsters who really got into the swing of things. Setting off briskly, they would enthusiastically cast aloft fistfuls of rose petals, their little hands reaching again and again into their baskets with astonishing speed. This was a fun new game, at the centre of a big crowd of admiring adults. By the time they were two-thirds of the way down the aisle, their baskets were empty. A thick, clumpy tapestry of rose petals trailed behind them—a cleaning nightmare for those patient staff coming through with vacuum cleaners afterwards.

At last, everybody would make it to the front. We would stop the music, and all eyes would turn to the celebrant.

For the flower girls and page boys, the fever of excitement ceased abruptly at that moment. Suddenly, they weren't the centre of attention anymore.

They had to stand still, for what felt like hours and hours while the ceremony droned on, with nobody to talk to and nothing to do.

They would get really, really, excruciatingly bored.

The early signs showed in shuffling feet, cavernous yawns, and curious stares being cast all around the venue and at the sea of faces.

Next, we would see little fingers excavating noses.

Some children would choose this time to begin a new game, which often involved vigorously swinging their flower basket. If there were any rose petals still inside, these would next be pulled out, inspected closely, then randomly distributed around the floor.

Some little girls carrying posies would start deconstructing them, flower by flower. Then they might attempt to fix them up again by poking the loose bits back in. Embarrassed adult bridesmaids, trying to look the part for the camera by maintaining a determined smile in the direction of the bride, would valiantly pretend not to notice the chaos unfolding next to them. Eventually a red-faced mother would rush up to rescue the posy and child.

For some little ones, fed up with the whole proceedings, it was time to wander off to the safety of a parent's lap, in the congregation.

Frequently nowadays, the smallest members of the

wedding party are the children of the bride and groom. It's the most natural impulse in the world, when they're not sure what else to do, to head for a cuddle from mummy and daddy in the middle of the vows. Never mind mummy's beautiful long train and veil—just trample all over them in your shoes as you make a beeline for the safety of her arms.

During one ceremony, I spied among the wedding guests a cute little girl aged about three. She was dressed up in her best pink fairy outfit, complete with tiara, wand and wings, and was getting increasingly wriggly as the talking droned on. At last the celebrant was getting to the vows part.

"I need to go to the toilet," announced Fairy Wings, loudly and urgently.

"I do," responded the groom.

"I have to go NOW," wailed Fairy Wings desperately.

"I do," said the bride.

A red-faced mother hustled Fairy-Wings outside.

During the relaxed interval while the register was being signed, a much-relieved Fairy Wings and her mother returned to the milling crowd.

Fairy Wings had clearly had enough. She spent the last part of the ceremony blissfully asleep in her father's arms, wand discarded, looking rumpled and quite un-fairylike.

"Harold, don't do that," reproached a mother ineffectually, as her angel-faced child ripped yet another flower head off a shrub in the immaculate garden bed.

We were at one of the many private homes with large, manicured gardens that were hired out for weddings.

Harold was bored. He had no other children to play with, and during that pre-ceremony time, all the adults were busy talking grown-up talk. Down at Harold's altitude, the beckoning flower heads were an irresistible temptation for his busy fingers.

There's something about Mozart's bubbling major-key fast movements that unfailingly connects with young children. Mozart's music is by no means childish, but it has a transparency, innate joyfulness and sense of spontaneity that they instinctively respond to. Often, it makes them dance.

On this occasion, Mozart saved the day. As we played one of his *Divertimenti,* Harold, a shredded flower still in hand, noticed the music for the first time. His mouth dropped open. Entranced, he was drawn as if by a magnet, for a closer look.

A very close look indeed. He stood fixated, right at the elbow of our first violinist, Allison.

When we got to the end of the movement, Allison, who had been valiantly restricting her bow movements so as to avoid a collision with Harold's enquiring face, stopped and showed him the violin, giving him a little feel of plucking the strings.

His face lit up. Vandalising gardens forgotten, Harold had a special close encounter with music-making that day, which I hope he has never forgotten.

We were crammed into an uncomfortably small space in the semi-outdoor poolside area of a posh Gold Coast hotel. A late-afternoon summer storm was brewing outside. The day was humid enough, but the extra dampness around the pool was enervating.

Having gone hunting for suitable chairs for the quartet, I'd eventually tracked down a staffer who offered to locate some. "How many of you are there?"

The intimate gathering of family and friends all stood during the ceremony, wearing their wedding finery and clammily fanning themselves in the damp heat. Hemmed into our tiny corner, we musicians struggled to see through the press of sweating bodies to follow the ceremony and hear our cues.

The pool boasted an elaborate faux-rocky waterfall feature that doubled as a waterslide. The noise of its rushing waters caused the wedding guests to press in even more closely, in a vain attempt to hear what the celebrant was saying.

Several swimwear-clad holidaying couples lounged around

the sides of the pool. They were taking a keen interest in the free entertainment.

Their children, kitted out with snorkels, flippers, goggles and inflatable pool toys, were having a wonderful time in the water. They dived for treasures, staged mock battles and swimming races, and hurtled down the waterslide.

The ceremony was proving to be quite lengthy. Several family members had special readings to share, and many worthy words were spoken. But the speakers were difficult to hear, and many of the wedding guests were sneaking increasingly envious glances at the Snorkel Kids' antics in the water.

The photographer did her best to capture beautiful romantic shots of the bridal couple saying their vows and exchanging rings, against the backdrop of the waterfall.

But, back in a time long before the term "photobomb" had been thought of, the background of all their wedding photos would have featured bright pink, blue and green snorkels bobbing their way crookedly across the pool, flippers kicking wildly as a thrashing deep-dive was attempted, small bodies throwing themselves delightedly down the waterslide, and goggled faces with plastered-down pool hair, rising up out of the waters.

SO, HOW MANY OF YOU ARE THERE?

CHAPTER SIX

The Audience

There must be some subliminal trigger that goes off in the minds of arriving guests when they spot the musicians, seated in what we have judged to be a safely out-of-the-way spot with a good sightline to the celebrant.

Because that's exactly where they choose to stand: directly in front of us, completely blocking our sight-line, and backing into our bows while we play.

And then come the prams, strollers, and the occasional wheelchair. As the cellist, I have a particular difficulty because when playing my bow protrudes sideways, at a low height that tends to escape the notice of the unwary.

Following some unwritten law of the universe, wedding guests always decide to park their wheeled accessories right next to my seat in the quartet, thereby reducing the available walkway to the exact width of my bow. My resulting playing posture then becomes somewhat unconventional, as I have to keep executing a series of sideways lurches, at a precarious 45-degree angle with one foot in the air, to let people push past.

Over the years, I have developed quite an instinct for sensing an approaching pedestrian and can launch my sideways manoeuvre in unerring anticipation of their passage—another of that suite of specially honed, extra wedding skills that we string players develop.

Mostly this instinct serves me well. However, there was one wedding guest who caught me unawares with a stealthy approach from the rear, knocking my bow off the strings and almost out of my grip as he passed. Looking up at his departing profile, I recognised him. He was the Queensland Chief of Police.

A sizeable proportion of Queenslanders claim Irish ancestry, and we receive positive reactions whenever we play a selection of Irish tunes at receptions.

The best-known of these tunes is the *Londonderry Air*, otherwise known as *Danny Boy*. Whenever they hear it, wedding guests who have been showing no response whatsoever to our background music suddenly become all misty-eyed, pause in their conversations to listen, then thank us profusely for the nostalgic moment.

These reactions become somewhat exaggerated when the beer is flowing liberally. Many a tongue-loosened Aussie bloke fingers his green-hued tie lovingly as he ramblingly recounts his family's distant Hibernian connections.

At one Brisbane riverside venue, we were serenading the

guests during the pre-dinner hour, in a beautiful patio setting that gave onto lush gardens. A couple of waiters circulated with trays of not-very-substantial canapés, as the guests helped themselves generously to the liquid refreshments.

It was many hours since lunchtime, and the party was getting very jolly indeed as night fell.

Having garnered a clue from the bride's Irish family name, we decided it was time to break out the Irish tunes.

The reaction was instant and maudlin. Some of the ladies nodded, smiled, and sang along in wavering voices. Several closet Irishmen clutched their beer mugs lovingly to their chests as they enthusiastically bawled, off-key, the random few snatches of the lyrics that they actually knew.

One happily inebriated gent was having the time of his life. As we finished the song, he lurched over to us, and pulled out his wallet.

"Play it again!"

We scanned the faces of the other guests, not too sure if they'd be up for a repeat performance.

"I'll pay you, look, here's $25." He pulled notes out of his wallet and waved them at us.

"We're being paid to be here; we're not taking your money," I responded.

He grabbed my hand and pressed the notes into it.

"You're taking it—now play it again!" he roared jovially.

We complied.

Twice more, in fact. This was an unexpected financial bonus that was impossible to refuse without causing a scene.

As we ended the third rendition, our benefactor closed in clumsily to envelop each of us in a beery, nostalgic bear hug, each of us in turn doing our best to shield our instruments from his vice-like grip.

Receiving tips at a wedding is not quite the done thing, but in these circumstances, our Irish tunes really did help to get the party off to a rip-roaring start.

"The ceremony will be outside in the garden," explained the bride-to-be. And there's a gorgeous romantic balcony above it where we'll have the photos."

"And then we're using their function room for the reception," she added.

She had given me the address of a suburban pub and bottle shop.

I enquired whether she had a "Plan B" in case it rained.

She brushed it off. "We'll be right. Their gardens are beautiful."

The Big Day came, and the rain poured down incessantly.

Upon our early arrival, we were ushered through to the function room. In a hasty change of plans, the ceremony was to be held there, due to the inclement weather.

We looked around doubtfully. The plain, low-ceilinged room was painted an institutional, bland grey colour. The only lighting was unromantic fluorescent tubes.

The tables for the reception had been cleared out of the room to make space for the ceremony.

We commandeered four of the grey business-meeting-style chairs and set ourselves up in the corner.

The guests crowded noisily in.

The celebrant conducted the ceremony with determinedly bright cheerfulness, and the bridal couple appeared unfazed by the change of plans.

As soon as the ceremony was over and the newly-weds played out, the guests, who should have been mingling picturesquely in the outside garden setting, were instructed to instead make their way through to the public lounge bar for the hour-long interval before the reception.

The bridal couple were whisked away to do their photos indoors.

The function staff began hauling tables back in to re-set the room for the reception, as the last of the guests vacated.

What should the quartet do, we enquired, since we were engaged to play during this one-hour time period?

"We'll set you up in the bar too," was the breezy response from the function manager.

This was a first.

The public bar was already comfortably populated by the usual assortment of Saturday afternoon drinkers, pool players, and poker-machine punters. A TV blared from one corner with the weekend sportscast.

We stood uncertainly on the gaudily patterned carpet, as the wedding guests happily filed in and began ordering drinks. They evidently felt that their day had taken a turn for the better with this unexpected change of plans.

We were doubtful that our string music would be heard, or that it would even be welcomed, against the bleeping of the poker machines and the raucous roar of the TV sports.

But we had no choice. We had been paid to play during this hour, and then to play for the first part of the reception, so that was what we had to do.

At first, the patrons were somewhat bemused. Hearing string quartet music played in the public bar was a first for them too.

Valiantly serenading away in our corner, we chose what we hoped would be widely recognised tunes.

The reaction came when we began Handel's *Arrival of the Queen of Sheba*.

First, a shower of low-value coinage spattered onto the carpet in front of us. Laughter, cheers, and mock tips. We forced a smile, gritted our teeth, and played on.

Next appeared the first of the amateur conductors, wielding a pool cue. If Irish tunes bring out the maudlin singing of closet Irishmen, the *Arrival of the Queen of Sheba* never fails to rouse the hidden conducting aspirations of middle-aged gentlemen with pint in hand.

Before long, we had quite a crowd. Clearly attracted by the novelty of the situation, they provided a noisy commentary as we played. Several of them took turns at conducting with the pool cue, and the banter became extremely good-natured.

In this way the hour passed, and the guests began returning to the function room for the reception. Hastily packing our instruments to relocate there too, we paused to gather up our tips from the carpet. Hardly a lucrative profit, but not one to be passed up, either. We figured it was hardship money.

Brisbane's Tattersalls Club was Brisbane's sanctuary for moneyed professional gentlemen. Upon entering its sleek, ground floor lift foyer, we began to breathe the rarefied air of true luxury.

Females weren't often granted access to the male bastion into which we emerged when the lift doors opened. Thick, sound-absorbing carpet, high ceilings, ornate plasterwork, old polished wooden doors, brass fittings, subtle lighting, leather lounge chairs, uniformed staff—the epitome of conservative exclusivity.

Clattering out of the lift with our instruments and music stands, we explained to the concierge, "We're the string quartet for the wedding function. Where should we set up for the pre-dinner drinks hour, please?"

He vaguely waved us in the direction of the bar area.

We asked if we might please use some chairs.

"How many do you need?" came the bored response, as he flicked his eyes over the four of us.

We chose a spot in the corner near the bar, as far as possible out of the traffic route of the busy wait-staff.

By now the lift doors were steadily disgorging a large crowd of expensively dressed wedding guests, who populated the bar and lounge area, chatting convivially.

Our classical music was perfect for the dignified setting. The guests enthusiastically topped up their glasses, mingled and socialised.

When the hour had nearly elapsed, we struck up the *Arrival of the Queen of Sheba*.

Almost immediately, a portly, beaming, dinner-suited gent materialised in front of us, majestically waving his arm in wide, conductor-like gestures.

He was joined by several more penguin-suited, red-cheeked chaps. They chortled, raised their glasses, and joined in the amateur conducting display.

Sensing that Handel was the man of the moment, we continued with the overture from his *Royal Fireworks* music, to loud vocal approval and more genial arm-waving.

Effusive applause from the gentlemen followed. Heads turned in the room, and several other guests clapped mildly, sensing that the occasion called for a response, even though they weren't quite sure what they were supposed to be applauding.

There were no monetary tips proffered on this occasion. But at least we had the satisfaction of being thanked and complimented by many of the guests as they filed into their reception.

The corporate sales conference dinner happened to be on State of Origin night. This is the Rugby League competition that even non-sports-fans like me are keenly aware of.

Well, you can't ignore it in this part of Australia, actually. Tribalism erupts vociferously at all levels of society, as the New South Wales and Queensland teams wage their annual battle for State supremacy. Outlandish costumes in team colours are cheerfully sported by young and old, as each of the three Origin games is celebrated vocally and boozily at venues and in front of TVs all over town.

Playing for the conference pre-dinner drinks, we were positioned on a balcony outside a Gold Coast resort's public lounge, within which a TV was relaying the game at high volume.

Feeling that the organisers might have wasted their money by having a string quartet up against the strong competition of the rugby league, we felt very lonely setting up on our balcony.

But it was one of those beguiling Queensland winter nights of cold, starry-splendoured clarity. We played happily, for our own enjoyment if nobody else's, only slightly distracted by the noise from the TV inside.

It wasn't long before guests began drifting outside. Attracted by the fresh air and the chance to chat, they formed a congenial group.

Glasses were topped up, the voices got louder, and the gathering on the balcony became very convivial indeed.

They began making requests.

Smoke on the Water is an old chestnut. I obliged with the bass riff, at least.

Then we played an arrangement of Louis Armstrong's *Wonderful World*. One young sales rep did a remarkably convincing gravelly-voiced rendition, to laughter and loud cheers. The party turned into a beery singalong.

To everything else that we played, they bopped along, sang, commented and cheered.

More guests were drawn outside to the epicentre of the party fun.

The Origin game on TV was mostly abandoned. The winners that night were Gershwin, Mozart, Handel, the Beatles, Vivaldi, and Louis Armstrong.

Upon arrival at the imposing two-storeyed clubhouse of the suburban golf course, a sign informed us that the wedding ceremony was to be on the lawn to one side of the building.

We set up on the downside of the gently sloping site, chairs wobbling on the not-quite-level, deep spongy turf.

On this glorious, sunny, autumn Saturday morning, the shadows were still long. The air hummed with birdcalls and the suburban sounds of lawnmowers and traffic.

The mostly youngish crowd gathered. Blokes in smart-casual gear gazed longingly at the sparsely populated golf links down the hill. Ladies in tight minidresses teetered on alarmingly high heels.

The ceremony proceeded over a background buzz of conversational sounds emanating from the overlooking first floor balcony. A large group of golfing types had emerged from the members' bar within, drinks in hand and enjoying the morning ambience.

The stillness of the spoken vows was abruptly shattered.

"Sssshhh, they're gettin' married," announced a large bloke on the balcony, in a stentorian voice.

"Whaat? ... Oh."

A happy crowd gathered, leaning over the balcony railings to watch the proceedings. This was a bonus sideshow for their weekly golf gathering.

The customary applause for the couple's first kiss was enthusiastically taken up with a round of loud cheers and whistles from the spectator's gallery.

If the level of public participation was a barometer for the success of the couple's wedding celebrations, this one was a triumph.

"You look just like Daphne," observed a florally dressed matron to me, as she clutched her wine glass and plate of hors-d'oeuvres. She had paused in her earnest conversation with a friend, to watch us as we played.

I was puzzled.

"Daphne?"

A faint bell began tinkling in the back of my mind. The film *Hilary and Jackie,* based on the memoir about the world-famous cellist Jacqueline du Pré by her sister Hilary, had recently been a box-office hit.

"Perhaps you mean Jacqueline du Pré … Jackie?", I offered.

"No, it was definitely Daphne."

Now, I do not remotely resemble Jacqueline du Pré in looks or mannerisms, and certainly not in skill. But I guessed that this lady had never seen anybody playing the cello. That is, until she watched that movie.

"Yes, she married some Jewish boy," mused the matron, with a faraway romantic gaze.

"Indeed," I replied pointedly. "She married Daniel Barenboim, a world-famous pianist and conductor."

But she had lost interest. Her eyes were already roving around the rest of the guests, looking for her next conversation partner.

We were set up on a luxurious green lawn, under the shade of a lush, spreading fig tree outside a large private home belonging to the bride's parents.

The usual assortment of relatives, friends of the parents, and friends and colleagues of the bridal couple stood around the manicured gardens, chatting in small groups while we played background music.

A couple of dour folk stomped doggedly around in full Welsh national dress, despite the Brisbane heat. I gathered that quite a contingent of hitherto-unmet relatives of the bride had flown in from various distant places for the event.

The mood seemed relaxed as the celebrant called everybody into position. But I was beginning to get the impression that the organisation of the bride's and groom's Big Day had not been entirely within their control.

The groom, clearly terrified, stood rigidly to attention, flanked by the best man and groomsman.

We played for the bride's mother to make her special entrance.

Sallying forth in stately fashion, she reached her seat, then faced about to check that all the cast and crew of this bridal pageant were correctly deployed. She watched approvingly as the bridesmaids entered with nervously measured slow steps, moving self-consciously to their designated spots.

The bride arrived on her father's arm, wide-eyed and pale-faced with stress.

Despite the couple's obvious nerves, the celebrant delivered a friendly ceremony that went down very well with the assembled guests.

But while the celebrant spoke, the groom kept up an unhappy muttered commentary to the bride: "Who are all these people? I've never met most of them. No idea who they are."

After the ceremony, the tension eased somewhat. The bride's large family contingent had their group photos with the newly-weds, while the other guests enjoyed the wine and finger-food that were being handed around.

Amongst the guests was a sizeable group of psychiatric nurses who all worked at the local hospital. They were enjoying our music, and I chatted with some of them as we played.

They expressed a tinge of disappointment with the day. It transpired that they had hatched a brilliant plan to honour the bridal couple in their own unique way. But they could not understand why the hospital had been uncooperative in refusing to provide them with the needed props to carry it out.

They had wanted to form a guard of honour, all of them

holding medical syringes triumphantly aloft.

Monty the Scots terrier was primped and coiffed, and looking photogenic in his special tartan ribbon, in honour of his adoring humans' Big Day.

We were playing background music in the courtyard of the couple's home, under a quaint pergola festooned with climbing roses. Monty was in his element, roaming interestedly around the paving stones and gravelled areas, sniffing at the large pots containing splendid flowering shrubs, and making friends with the assembled guests as they mingled sociably.

The lure of the four captive, seated humans in the string quartet proved irresistible. Monty trotted a happy circuit around our four chairs, tail thumping against our legs.

He developed a particular fascination for my cello spike, sniffing curiously at it as we played. Hoping that he would not mistake it for some kind of tree, I tried to ignore him, wondering why it is that with unerring instinct, dogs always pick on a "cat person" as the recipient of their loving attention.

But Monty was soon diverted.

Our viola player that day was a university student called Danielle. She loved dogs, and had utterly lost her heart to Monty's charms, murmuring endearments and reaching down to pat him whenever she had a few rest bars as we played.

The first time Monty put his paws up on her lap in response, she smothered him with delighted affection.

That settled it. Monty had found his new best friend.

Danielle was wearing a rather short skirt that day, and in a show of undying love, Monty licked her exposed knees adoringly.

She played on resolutely despite the distraction, as Monty stayed at his post with paws on her lap, licking at her knees with a blissful doggy grin, and being rewarded with giggles and pats.

Monty tried his best to steal the show, but Danielle never missed a beat.

CHAPTER SEVEN

Tributes

Over the years, we have worked regularly with some wonderful celebrants. They each have their own style and idiosyncracies.

Celebrants are expert multi-taskers. They must simultaneously support emotional brides, stage manage excited participants who have forgotten where to stand, deliver their script flawlessly, wrangle all manner of extra props that have been employed to create special moments within the ceremony, and work the crowd to keep them involved in the proceedings.

Celebrants, like musicians, battle the elements at outdoor venues. They have to hang onto flyaway paperwork whilst juggling microphones to make their voices carry over wind, traffic, and other background noise.

Whenever we musicians have difficulty hearing what a celebrant is saying, the cue points within the ceremony become a little tricky, especially when our sight-line is also obscured as the guests crowd around. We need to watch for when the bride arrives at the front after walking in, and to see when the signing is completed and the celebrant is lining up the wedding party again in preparation for announcing the newly married couple.

We appreciate those celebrants who take a few moments to chat with us beforehand about how they are going to manage those all-important cues: most of all the signal for when the bride is ready to enter, and the cue for when we should begin the exit processional music.

These moments aren't always as straightforward as they seem.

Most celebrants make the bride's entry cue crystal clear by asking the guests to stand. Others just ever-so-slightly incline their head in the direction of the quartet, with an ambiguously raised eyebrow that we hesitantly interpret as our signal to play.

After the register is signed, we wait for those immortal words, "I present to you Mr and Mrs ...." But this is always worth checking with the celebrant beforehand. On a few occasions, we have launched into the triumphal exit music at that phrase, only to be forced into an embarrassed *pianissimo* a few seconds later, when a celebrant decides to interrupt the congratulatory buzz with a further announcement that they just thought of.

And then there are the extra accessories brought in to add just the right touch to the ceremony.

Celebrants have to remain unflappable when tablecloths, quill pens and certificates develop a mind of their own on windy days, when candles prematurely blow out, or when doves and butterflies fail to fly romantically aloft on cue.

Or when rings stubbornly refuse to come untied from the cute little cushions on which they have been presented, or get dropped by nervous fingers through a deck's timber boards into the muddy waters beneath.

Celebrants have to proceed calmly over the excited antics of pet dogs who behave less than impeccably in their role as ring-bearers by running away with the rings.

We watched one celebrant maintain admirable poise when a large eagle, having flown straight and low up the aisle to bear the rings to a gauntlet-wearing groom, made an unscheduled detour over the guests' heads for a peck around the venue's gardens, instead of obediently returning to its handler.

A beautiful practitioner of the celebrant's art was Barbara Reynolds Hutchinson, with whom we developed a good friendship over many years. We loved her genuineness, joyfulness and thoughtfulness, as well as her thorough professionalism.

It was Barbara who had the best technique of efficiently gathering the guests in readiness for the bride's arrival. She did this by rehearsing them for their active participation in the moment when they would be asked, as friends and family, if they would be an ongoing support to the couple.

Barbara was determined that their response, "We will," would be delivered promptly and with gusto. She would get them to practise several times beforehand until they really got into the spirit of it.

At her ceremonies, the moment when the resounding "We will" burst forth was always a highlight and the trigger for delighted laughter.

I have been blessed in the rich friendships I have made with wonderful musicians, over many years of sharing the specialness of unconventional experiences, laughter, and lots of music. It is a great privilege to earn a little extra money having so much fun.

Our mostly classical repertoire is humbling and wonderful. I never tire of the music, which is fresh and different every time we play it, and I laugh with the sheer joy of it.

We get to interact with a richly varied cast of guests, bridal parties, celebrants, photographers, and those innocent members of the public who occasionally provide a fascinatingly incongruous byplay as we face the vagaries of venues and the elements.

We've played at all sorts of indoor and outdoor venues. They may have limited lighting, blazing sunshine or wind-funnelling outdoor terraces—but they have wonderful, if harried, staff.

We've perched on church pews, tables, upended crates, organ benches, rickety fold-up chairs, deck chairs, and cheap, spine-curling plastic chairs.

We've played on sandy shores, hillsides, soggy lawns, paddocks and boats, and in homes, clubs, churches, restaurants and community halls.

What a privileged, if unconventional way of getting to know the many facets of our beautiful city, Brisbane.

I had the special richness of sharing the music with my late mother, who played first violin in the quartet for four years.

She had been a professional violinist in the New Zealand Symphony Orchestra throughout her working life. Then, after moving to Queensland, she was a member of the Queensland Symphony Orchestra for four years before retiring. Our quartet playing was not only a means of earning a little extra income, but also became a special opportunity for Mum and me to spend time together.

After some odd hiccups occurred in her otherwise excellent health, my mother was diagnosed with breast cancer. She underwent surgery and further treatment, but the cancer had already spread to her liver.

Mum kept playing in the quartet during that year, for as long as she was physically able.

Throughout six months of chemotherapy, she approached our gigs with indomitable enthusiasm and laughter.

The last couple of times we played together were in a piano

trio. We had been asked to perform at a special event for the Hungarian community on the Gold Coast. My mother's neighbour, Imre, was passionate about the romance of Léhar's music and had scripted a narrated presentation.

He really summed it up about Mum, with a word all of his own.

In raptures over the way she caught the lilt and the upswing of this sweeping, romantic music, he conflated the noun and past participle forms of the German word for "swing" in paying her his highest compliment.

"You got geschwungen," he enthused in his thick Hungarian accent.

Mum did indeed have geschwungen—not only in her playing, but in the buoyant, positive way she approached all of life.

Joan, our original viola player, had founded the quartet. Having taken up the viola late in life, she was passionate about her playing, and her myriad other musical and community involvements.

I knew that Joan had admired my mum's will and stamina during the months of playing quartet gigs whilst she underwent chemotherapy.

Nine years later, it was Joan's turn.

For several months, Joan had been unable to shake off a

persistent, nagging cough.

On a shimmeringly sunny day redolent with the perfume of roses, we finished playing for a morning wedding in a park rotunda. I walked beside Joan out along the short path to where our cars were parked.

She was moving very slowly and puffing for breath. The others had gone on ahead.

Abruptly, she stopped walking and stooped to put her case and bag down, gasping, "I need to rest for a minute."

Joan then confided that she had just been diagnosed with lung cancer. This was a shock, as she had never been a smoker. With her boundless optimism, she wanted to keep the news private until treatment options had been explored.

Her face was blanched, with a cold sweat on her brow. I recognised the same cancer-induced exhaustion that used to regularly overtake my mum during the last months of her life.

That was when I knew that Joan only had months to live. She was determined to keep making memories for as long as she could.

Six months later, she played with us for the last time. By then, she was under palliative care at her home. We were providing one hour of informal outside music for a local church's Christmas lights display, and Joan was adamant that she would play.

That evening was clear and magical, with a heavy fragrant scent of tropical flowers on the light breeze. The stars framed the man-made sparkle of the Christmas lights all around us. A jolly crowd of sightseers wandered around, many sitting for a while to listen. Excited children sang and danced along to the carols that we had included in our set.

Joan played on and on. By the end of the hour, her left elbow was resting on her knees to support the weight of her viola, but still she refused to stop.

She was drinking in every sound, every sight, every sensation.

Joan died two weeks later.

Postlude: Bagatelle
(Just for fun)

The next generations of string quartet players are out there somewhere. Maybe they are already studying the violin, viola or cello, or maybe they are struggling along with a different instrument entirely.

All parents whose children show the remotest interest in music go through the agonies of trying to work out which instrument their child should begin learning.

The piano is an obvious choice, and a sensible one, as it gives excellent foundational skills in understanding chords, and in reading music. It lays out visually how the notes step in relation to each other, as they are heard. Because the notes are produced mechanically as the keys are touched, the finer points of learning to play in tune don't apply, whilst other musical skills are being acquired. And, the piano is a useful, versatile instrument for providing accompaniments in a variety of settings.

However, I know too many people who were permanently scarred by the old-style "rap-'em-over-the-knuckles" piano teaching methods. Childhood enthusiasm ruined, they made a lifetime decision that music wasn't for them. This is tragic, and too often people in their adult years get a serious attack of the might-have-beens.

Or sometimes, they just started out on an instrument for which they didn't feel any affinity. The solution could have been as simple as finding a different instrument that suited them better.

I have observed, from long experience in playing for theatre shows in backstage orchestra pits where the audience can't see the players, how different are the personalities of the various instrument types.

The three main groups—strings, woodwind, and brass—are all so disparate that they might as well have come from different planets. The pianists and drummers add a dimension all of their own.

After playing for many long show seasons, during which multiple bags of peppermint lollies did the rounds of the backstage orchestra pit, I had a flash of inspiration.

It's what people do with their Mintie papers that's the real give-away.

The string players get feverishly busy with the "tear the Mintie paper into a long thin strip" competition, then festoon the results artistically about, all the time chatting and giggling hysterically (quietly of course, for in a backstage pit, each instrument is miked). There's always an origami expert who creates wondrous, tiny, masterpieces with their Mintie papers, then presents them to other players to use for decoration.

Brass players make pea-shooters, using their balled-up Mintie papers as deadly missiles. Or they stuff them creatively into ears, noses, eye sockets, or into each other's instruments—whilst making as many extraordinary oral sound effects as they can think of and squirting their instrument lubricants liberally in all directions.

Woodwind players sit quietly, independently, each in splendid withdrawn isolation, frequently with their noses in a book or gazing neutrally at the frenetic goings on all around them. With their central location in the orchestra pit, they really are the calm eye of the hurricane. They place their Mintie papers neatly at their feet. If they do decide to participate in the general Minties mayhem, they may surreptitiously donate their Mintie paper, with just the barest glimmer of a smile, to another player to do something with.

Drummers throw their Mintie papers into the two-foot-deep pigsty growing around their drum kit—the happy accumulation of discarded score pages, fizzy-drink cans, and takeaway food remains. Morosely glaring at the brass players, they duck the occasional wayward missile that finds its way through their protective thicket of cymbals.

Pianists are truly laid back, and their thoughts are on another planet. They may participate in the missile throwing with a sudden energetic burst of community spirit, or they may just chuck their Mintie papers messily away and go back to their own little world.

And so my Theory of Selecting the Right Instrument has developed. In order to determine which musical instrument a particular child might be gifted for, you could put all the children in a room, give them each a Mintie, and watch what they do with their Mintie papers.

Acknowledgements

Special mention to my long-time string quartet buddies and friends Andrea Slater, Marie Herzig, Allison Stenning and Alison Harbottle, for so many years of fun and hilarity playing together at gigs and concerts. I treasure each of you.

In memory of my mum Sandra Averi, and of the founder of our quartet, Joan Bevan.

Thanks to Bridget Gunn, and to my father Peter Averi, who read through my manuscript and gave me helpful feedback.

And, thanks to all the other musicians, brides and grooms, celebrants, and ever-so-patient staff at so many venues, who have all been part of our quartet's long and colourful story.

Alex Averi

Printed in Great Britain
by Amazon

42614347R00069